Tales from North Bay & Beyond:
More Bear Spring Camps Stories

Joseph M. Kockelmans

DEDICATION

To David Trost and his wonderful family, wife Geri, and daughters Ashley and Emily. David, you are and always will be my buddy and brother.

To Mrs. Marguerite Mosher.

And to all the campers I have known throughout my life who are still on earth, but unable to join us at Bear Spring.

CONTENTS

ACKNOWLEDGMENTS

To Bertram and Marguerite Mosher. To their daughters Jane, Lynn, Martha, and Peg, and their families. Since 1910, with their gracious hospitality and their caring nature, the Moshers and Churchills have been giving campers a wonderful place to enjoy their yearly vacations.

To Jeremy and Amanda Lindstrom, and their son, Landon. Jeremy contributed to my story about the seaplane ride over the Belgrade chain of lakes. Thank you, Jeremy.

To the Dunn family.

To the Comick family.

To Rick Bennett, and to his sister, Kathy.

And to the many, many families who come to Bear Spring Camps throughout the season.

MY MOM'S TYPICAL DAY AT BEAR SPRING CAMPS

My mother, Dr. Dorothy Greiner Kockelmans, enjoyed a much more laid-back experience at Bear Spring than David Trost and I did. As where Dave and I would rush off to go fishing with Uncle Cy Greco, Mom stayed at the dining hall to enjoy that second cup of coffee of the morning.

On the way in to breakfast, Mom would put two quarters in the payment bowl on the porch and take her morning paper, a copy of the Waterville *Morning Sentinel*. While waiting for our breakfast order, she would quickly glance at such things like the day's weather forecast and what page her puzzles were on. Sometimes Dave and I would ask her to read us our horoscopes.

Mom never walked up to meals as long as I knew her. Even on bright sunny days, she would drive up to the main house in her 1976 Cadillac Sedan Deville, purchased by Grandmother, and in later

1

years, in her 1987 Lincoln Town Car. When she had her fill of coffee and was ready, she would collect her sunglasses, paper, and keys and would drive down to the camp.

Mother enjoyed her porch immensely. She would grab a pen from inside, take a seat on one of the camp's porch chairs, and begin to work her crossword puzzle. As crosswords were one of my mother's hobbies, it usually didn't take her very long to finish. After that, she would begin to work the word jumble puzzles. Those are my personal favorites. More times than not, she would leave at least one or two words for me. Not that she couldn't figure out the words; she just knew that both Dave and I liked to contribute.

At 10 a.m. or thereabouts, rain or shine, Mom would always take a trip into Belgrade Lakes. To get what, you ask? That's right, more papers. She would occasionally pick up cherry Twizzlers, which she called twists. She would also say hello to the people who worked at Day's store. She would try to return back to camp by 11:30, thus giving her an hour to work at least one of her crosswords. Around this time, the *Galileo* would be pulling back into the dock. Stories of the whoppers we let go would be bragged about, and pre-dinner beverages would be served; sodas for David and me and an Old Grand-Dad whiskey with water and ice for Mom. Sometimes, I would catch my mother smiling, and she would tell me that she had waited all year to sit on her porch, hold her drink, and enjoy looking at *her* lake.

When dinner time rolled around, we would all again be the 'firstest of the first.' Instead of having hot coffee mid-day, Mom usually brought up a Pepsi from the cabin refrigerator. She was funny up at Bear Spring. Back home she preferred tea or Coca-Cola. At camp though it was always Pepsi. Mom looked forward to not only the breakfast meal but also to dinner. As *I* lived for Bear Spring's oatmeal, Mom lived for Sunday Chicken with all the trimmings, and blueberry pie with vanilla ice cream.

We would all get back down to the lake around 2:00. Mom would take her time freshening up after the meal before coming out to relax on the porch. If she decided to wade in the lake that day, she would put on her bathing suit. She would either sit on one of the porch chairs or lounge on the hammock. This was her ultimate relaxation time. Mom had waited all year to gaze at the lake. Somehow it rejuvenated her as it did all of us. Around 2:30 or so, Dave and I would break her restful silence by announcing that it was time for the daily boat ride. We would always ask her if she wanted to join us and every so often she would. Most times however she would say, "You boys go on and have fun."

Back when my mom's crowd was still going to Bear Spring, the happy hour was still in full force. Mom would always freshen up, put on some slacks and some make-up, before heading to the appropriate cabin for the happy hour gathering. Everyone seemed to know what my mom liked to drink; she really only liked one alcoholic beverage. Mom and her friends would be on the porch, mingling. Always a tasty variety of snacks and goodies would be there for the offing. Her favorite was cheese and crackers. When supper rolled around at

6:00, my mother always went (meals were already paid for), but on happy hour evenings she would eat light.

On cool evenings, of which there were a few even in early August, Mother might arrange wood, paper and kindling in the fireplace for the morning, so it could be lit quickly if needed. If it was a warmer night, she would sit on her porch and star-gaze or watch the moon on the lake.

When Dave and I would return from our early evening fishing trip, Mom would drive us down to Waterville in the car to enjoy an ice cream cone, a game of miniature golf, or a few games of candle pin bowling. When at Rummel's ice cream parlor, every once in a great while, we would hear our favorite song on the radio through the outdoor speaker system. It was Percy Faith's "Theme from *A Summer Place.*" That song has special meaning for me and even more for my mother. I think it was one of her favorite movies.

On the way home from Waterville, Mother would switch on WGAN-FM radio. Dave and I would be filled with sugary ice cream and Mom would want soft, soothing easy listening music to help calm us down. We'd return back to camp about 9:30 or so. After Mom spent so much of the day outside on the porch in the warm summer sun and breeze, she would quickly be off to bed, leaving Dave and I to play a couple of quick quiet games of either Yahtzee or cards. She would wake up again the next morning to enjoy her next typical day at Bear Spring Camps.

BASKETFUL OF LIFE AT CAMP TALES

The New Kockelmans Cabins - In 2009, I made my grand re-entrance to Bear Spring Camps. I was told ahead of time that I would no longer have my mom's cabin; the one I loved. Deep down, I kind of figured that, so it wasn't a big shock. Peg and I had discussed a one-bedroom cabin that she was certain I would like. It was the second to last on the other side of the bridge. As I remember it, four or five steps lead up to a porch which had a nice safe railing. There were beautiful trees and bushes in front, but a dock that did not look safe for me to walk down because of my bad balance.

When I went into the cabin for the first time, a smile instantly came upon my face. The cabin resembled a studio apartment where everything was in one room. The living room area was to the left side of the cabin while the beds were to the right. There were enough windows to make it well-lit even though it was nestled in the woods. In the back of the cabin was the bathroom, as well as a small walk-in closet. The first year back I came by bus, so I didn't have a whole lot to unpack. After about thirty minutes or so I was ready to sit on my porch for the first time. I took special note of how different the view of the lake was. I was looking straight at Snake Point, not at Otter and Oak islands as I would from Mom's camp.

This was the first time ever that I would sit on my porch, look at the lake and have no one to talk to. Mom was gone and the only week I could get back was not David's. Dan and Chris Harvey, part of David's wife's family, were the only people I knew. After a short while, I made my way down to their cabin, where I kept company the rest of the afternoon until supper.

Having meals with them at their table was comforting. Granted I enjoyed being back, but there were far too many unfamiliar faces. Just a few of my mom's second week crowd were there. Most of her bunch had either passed away or stopped coming. That evening I plugged in the small portable radio that I had brought and tried to find some music that resembled the style I had enjoyed years ago. No instrumental stations could be found and I could only take country music for so long.

I vividly remember using the propane heater which Mother had never allowed; she called it cheating. "Just throw on another cover if you are cold," she'd say. But no, this was my cabin. I was going to do what I wanted. While sitting in the living room area, I would usually set the heater on setting 2, giving the living room a nice, even warmth without making it too hot or stuffy. When I went to sleep, however, if it was a cool night, I would switch it to setting 3 or 4. I hated to be cold.

During the week there were at least two evenings that I invited the Harveys down to keep me company. We told stories, laughed, and built bonfires. Even though I tried to make friends that first year, somehow it seemed tough. I suppose I was trying to get into what I later called my routine. I was no longer a follower; I was the leader and head of my camp.

That first year back after my three year absence, I do vividly remember taking nothing for granted. I absolutely savored every second; the week felt like a month. As I would walk to breakfast slowly, I paid special attention to the chirping birds, the breeze rustling the leaves and any chatter of folks sitting on their porches. On the one morning that it rained, Dan Harvey came down in his car and picked me up. He and his wife went out of their way to make certain that I was well taken care of and didn't feel like the person on the outside looking in.

In 2010, I was fortunate enough to get back to Bear Spring on David's week. I was going to have another new cabin, four or five camps closer to his, and I was thrilled. Unbeknownst to me, I was going to have the camp right next to the one my mom started with in her early years, called *Sunshine*. Mine was *Sunshine North*. With a wall separating the living room and bedroom, the camp had a slightly smaller feel to it, though I think the size was pretty much the same as the one I had the year before. With comfortable furniture and a good bed, I certainly had everything I needed to be happy there.

My view of the lake was more like what I grew up with. I still couldn't quite see Otter Island, and Oak Island was out of the question. More of North Bay was visible, that was for certain, and the more I could see the more I liked it.

Something unpleasant happened in 2010. I suffered my first injury while on vacation. While loading the fridge with soda and beer, I bent down a little too far or too quickly, and when I stood up, I felt pain in the back of my left leg. Walking down steps was awkwardly slow and sitting on the plastic porch chairs gave me an excruciating pinch in the hip area. I'm not certain what I did, but I probably stretched my hamstring. Simple things like getting in and out of chairs, getting dressed and walking up to the dining hall were a chore.

The fishing gods must have been laughing at me that year for two reasons. First, getting in and out of the camp boat was painful. I could only fish without discomfort when in the pontoon boat, which was level with the dock and easier to get into. Second, when did my leg heal? … the day before I was to leave!

This past summer I brought more stuff with me in a rented car. When I went to plug in my radio, however, I found out that there was no outlet where I really wanted one. The radio had to sit on top of the fridge.

I try to make the new cabin my own. What do I mean by that? Well, when I was younger, Mom and Dad would sometimes walk in to the old camp and find that previous campers changed some furniture around, or perhaps they had moved the small refrigerator from one spot to another. This past year, my cabin had a slightly different look than it did the first year I had it. I didn't want to run the risk of hurting myself by moving pieces of furniture, so I just left everything right where it was. Now granted, if there had been anything that I truly didn't like, such as my favorite chair had been moved into the bedroom, I certainly would have asked a cabin boy to help move it back where I wanted it.

I'm not certain whether my friend Dave and family "make the camp the way they want it," as my mom used to say, but for me, if everything functions, no lights are burned out, and the propane gas heater works, I am quite satisfied.

I remember how nice it felt to be fishing with David and his family again. They had all graduated to pontoon boat fishing which was certainly more comfortable, roomier, and it was easier for me to keep my balance. I found out very quickly that David still had the knack for fishing. The young teenagers would be content using worms to try to catch white perch, while Dave and I went after big bass. Talking with him in the back of the pontoon brought back memories and a glimpse of the old days. It felt like Mom might just be waiting for us on the porch.

Great Pond from Above - A Bear Spring Camps tradition that I have always wanted to partake of, though fear has kept me from it, is going in the sea plane for the tour of the Belgrade chain of lakes. I'd always wanted to try it, but wasn't particularly fond of the tiny aircraft they used. I'm quite certain that it was perfectly safe, but I much prefer a Boeing 737 or 747 as my mode of flight.

Since early childhood, I have indeed been fascinated by aircraft. My family and I used to travel to Europe on big jumbo jets. I suppose I just feel safer than in a little Cessna. I have seen them depicted on films and TV shows, in particular on an episode of *Emergency!*, where paramedics John Gage and Roy DeSoto had to rescue some people from a disabled Cessna. When the passenger door was opened, it looked just a little bit bigger than a walk-in pantry. That's too small for me.

Many of my friends have taken the tour. As I recall, it lasted about twenty minutes and traveled over Great Pond, East Pond, Long Pond, North Pond, and Messalonskee. Everyone who I have ever talked to has loved the trip. I think years ago it cost around fifteen or twenty dollars. I have no idea what they charge today, if the trip is even still offered.

The aircraft was a Cessna 182 or similar model, and probably held four to five passengers. A good friend of mine, Jeremy Lindstrom, has taken this ride on at least one occasion. Since he has taken the sea plane flight, I asked him to contribute a couple of paragraphs for this book detailing his experience. He shared his memory of a trip he took with his wife, Amanda. I have edited his writing for grammar and spelling but not for content.

We had been going to Bear Spring Camps for several years, and for the first time we were staying a few days into the 'second week' that Amanda had attended for many years as a child. As her generation grew older and lives became busier, everyone stopped attending the second week with the exception of her immediate family. After moving to Illinois, Amanda and I hadn't been able to visit Bear Spring Camps for two weeks, but this would be the year we would stay a few extra days.

I hadn't seen a seaplane at Great Pond until that year, and it turned out he was landing due to the low fuel level on his plane. We assisted him in filling his spare tanks at the local gas station, and he offered a '2 for 1' deal as a way of thanking us. We didn't have much time before heading to supper, but we took him up on the offer.

Taking off on the lake was a truly amazing experience; a combination of racing to Otter Island by boat and taxiing down the runway to your favorite vacation spot. The view of the Belgrade Lakes and surrounding area by air was breathtaking, particularly seeing the town of Belgrade since we were most familiar with taking trips from camp to Belgrade for souvenirs each year. We also spotted the local golf course along with the beauty of the Maine countryside, before setting our eyes on the familiar red roof of the dining hall, as we approached camp from a different angle than expected. We buzzed the entrance to camp as we quickly descended toward Great Pond for landing, as the other campers below were making their way to the dining hall for the perfect meal to end the perfect day.

It was a quick ride, but one that will last forever in the memory of anyone who enjoys the annual trip to Bear Spring Camps and the beauty of the August shade of green that is otherwise known as Maine.

In 1987 or so, Brandy Bennett and I were in the *Galileo* taking a video of North Bay scenery. I had asked Brandy, the camera person that day, to get good shots of camp, Snake Point, and all the pretty houses lining North Bay's shores. She happily agreed to do so. The added bonus that day was that the seaplane was taking off, giving campers rides for a couple of hours. Brandy captured the red and white plane on videotape and I still watch it to this day.

Jeremy has written that he has not seen the seaplane for a number of years. It may very well be true that that person or company no longer offers rides to Bear Spring Campers. Of that I am not certain. I have not seen the seaplane myself in a few years but I assumed that it was still done at some point during the summer. If I ever see the plane come again when I'm there and have the money to do it, I will throw caution to the wind and try it.

A Night at Aunt Marilyn's Cabin - In the 1970s, I had a rare opportunity to spend a night in another cabin. My mom's sister, my aunt Marilyn Greiner, and her two sons, Matt and Mike, got a cabin at Bear Spring for the first two weeks in August. My cousins were around my age, and together we had lots of fun fishing, swimming and boating. One evening, Aunt Marilyn invited me to spend the night at her place.

The cabin she rented was much bigger than Mom's. As I recall, it had a wrap-around porch and was set higher up off the ground.

After I climbed the five steps to the porch, Aunt Marilyn invited me in and gave me a tour. The cabin had three bedrooms and a nice sized living room. It was in a more wooded area situated almost at the end of the property. Mom came over and we sat around, told stories, and had a very pleasant evening.

When it was time to go to bed, I went to my room, the boys went to theirs, and Aunt Marilyn went to hers. As memory serves, it was lights out around 10:00. Matt and Mike liked to get up early to go fishing. We were going to go the next morning.

The night began as any other. I left my lamp on the side dresser lit for a while as I unwound. I reviewed the day's activities as I planned the next. I couldn't help but notice that the bed seemed to be wider than the one I was used to at my cabin. Around 11:00, I switched off the light and slowly drifted off to sleep.

A few hours later, I woke up just enough to know that I wanted to readjust my pillow, but lo and behold, I couldn't find it. The longer I searched, the stranger the moment became. Only a handful of times in my life was I so disoriented as to not know where I was. This night was one of these times. I couldn't find either of my pillows. Or the headboard. I was still on the mattress, so I knew I hadn't fallen out of bed. I went to switch on my lamp. It was not where it was supposed to be either. The trees outside made it considerably darker in the bedroom than I was used to. I needed to orient myself. After several minutes of patting around, I found the pillows.

Somehow, someway, I had almost completely turned my body around and was lying sideways on the mattress. So, after first sitting up, I found my night table, then the lamp, and once the light was on, I could quickly get my bearings again. A few seconds later, Aunt Marilyn called to me, asking if everything was all right. I felt a little bit embarrassed as I explained to her what had happened. She reassured me that that could easily happen in unfamiliar surroundings.

The next morning, I had breakfast at their table in the dining room. Not only did I want to thank Aunt Marilyn for having me at her cabin for the night, but also I wanted to discuss with the cousins where they wished to go fishing. We made our plans and were leaving, as Mom was making an unusually late appearance. She told me later that Aunt Marilyn explained what had happened to me the night before. Mom probably found it amusing.

Maine Song - In the 1980s, I made certain that one song each year had a special meaning during the two weeks at camp. I called it the "Maine Song." It was one song, usually on one of my cassette tapes, which passed one or both of my two criteria. I listened to music a lot all year, on the radio, on records, and on tapes. It made sense that it would filter into my camp life, too.

The first of my two criteria for the "Maine song" selection was if it was playing on my Sony Walkman at the time that our car passed over the Piscataqua River Bridge, at Kittery, Maine. There, halfway across, the Welcome to Maine sign came into view. This bridge linked New Hampshire with Maine. The actual state line used to be in the middle of this bridge. Today, I believe the state line has been moved several hundred yards so that the sign is actually on land, not over water. The sign read, "Welcome to Maine. Vacationland."

The second criterion was for when I wasn't able to listen to a song while going over the bridge. When Pop came with us, he would usually play his classical cassettes on the car's tape deck, making it difficult for me to hear my music, even under headphones. Yes, Dad liked his Mozart and Bach loud. If during the two week vacation there was one song that I listened to that stood out more than others, that would be the one that I chose.

The first Maine song was "We Are Family" by Sister Sledge from their 1979 cassette tape of their album of the same name. (This same year the Pittsburgh Pirates baseball team started using this song for the '79 season for their local TV broadcasts.) I was impressed that the song fit the camp experience so well – the people at Bear Spring Camps were, and still are, family to me. I would listen to that cassette at least once a day; usually before fishing. At the time I did not know that this would be the first of several.

Another Maine Song was Michael Jackson's "Beat It" from the cassette, *Thriller*. I remember back in 1983, I played that tape quite extensively. "Beat It and other songs such as "Billy Jean," "Thriller" and "The Girl Is Mine" reminded me of the camp experience that year. That particular year, when my mom and I left Pennsylvania, I only had room in the front seat of the car for my Walkman and about three tapes. Rather than juggling them every half-hour, I decided to play "Beat It" and "Billy Jean," the first two songs on the tape, over and over again. We weren't even into New York State and one of those songs already had the inside track for Maine Song, no pun intended. The second tape I had with me in the car was Peter Frampton's *Frampton Comes Alive!* "Something's Happening" and "Doobie Wah" were early serious contenders. If my memory serves, the third cassette was an audio fireside chat of Uncle Cy Greco. I think I only played it one time on the trip and had trouble hearing it so I put it away until we got to Bear Spring.

One year when just Mom, Dave, and I were at camp, we came down from breakfast. I had already loaded the tape in the player the night before, and we listened to the first side of Elton John's *Greatest Hits vol.1*, before going out to fish – "Rocket Man," "Daniel," "Honky Cat," "Goodbye Yellow Brick Road," and "Saturday Night is Alright for Fighting."

Other songs which made the list were "Celebrate!" by Cool and the Gang, "I Was Made for Lovin' You" by KISS, as well as Bruce Springsteen's entire cassette, *Born in the USA*. The very earliest Maine song, before the phrase even existed in my mind, was *All I Ever Need Is You* by Sonny and Cher. That has extra meaning to me, for it reminds me of a special friend, Patty Patrick. The two other songs I like from that cassette were "Here Comes that Rainy Day Feeling," and a version of "More Today than Yesterday."

By a fluke, the Maine song came back in 2011 when I took cassettes and a tape player to camp. I would wind down the evening with a Pepsi and side one of the KISS album *Creatures of the Night* before going to bed.

MY NEW TRADITIONS

Now that I have been back at Bear Spring for a few years, I have begun to develop my own way of doing things; my own daily routine. As a traditionalist, I always liked to keep to Mom's schedule and do the things the way we always did. We'd take my boat, the *Galileo*, out on the lake to enjoy a ride, before returning for a happy hour with friends before supper. Mom and I would also go to Waterville every evening for recreation; to visit Jiggs Mosher, to watch a half-hour of baseball over coffee at Killarney's pub at the old Holiday Inn, or to enjoy a small cup of ice cream at Gifford's.

My mother passed away and I was on my own. Times and people change. Due to a change in circumstances, I began to come up with some of my own new traditions while keeping a few of Mom's. I'm riding in someone else's boat when I am on the lake, my happy hours are solo, and I'm staying at camp in the evenings, going to bonfires.

One thing that will not change is my desire to be at the breakfast table come 7:30. The past few years I have sat with David and his family at their table. Being part of a large family now is nice in that it has afforded me the opportunity to open up more to everyone instead of sinking into a shell, which I had done after my divorce. If there is one drawback to not having my own table, it would be this: most mornings I like to have time to plan my day and to figure out what is going to happen tomorrow. Once folks start walking in, however, conversations about what happened the evening before fill the area. Usually, David and his wife Geri walk in first, followed by their daughters, Ashley and Emily. Geri likes to walk before breakfast and Dave is always up and eager to fish. The girls, however, don't seem to be morning people. Breakfast takes a little longer with so many people there. Dave and I no longer rush down to the dock and get out onto the lake.

The biggest thing that I miss, and I suppose you could call it a tradition, is my boat, the *Galileo*. We no longer have her to use for the morning fishing or the traditional afternoon boat ride. She gave us twenty-nine years of service and her best years were behind her. I was told she needed major repairs, which I could not afford. Now I rely on others to take me on the lake, which all in all is not too bad. I actually enjoy being pampered now and then on the bigger pontoon rental. Once in a while, though, I wish I was the captain again and, with David, could head out to the spots that *I* chose, on my own timetable.

Being alone has its disadvantages. If I wish to have a pre-dinner drink and Dave and family are busy, I find myself having a drink for one. It can be lonely, especially on a day that is gray, rainy, and dreary. On afternoons that Dave is busy, at the happy hour time I am again enjoying a beverage by myself. I have actually found myself looking at my watch and saying, yikes, still half an hour to supper. I am trying to recapture the old days, wishing that Mom was still here, as well as feeling silly being on the porch alone with my Pepsi, making certain that the entire happy hour has taken place before going up to supper. This is not every day though. My buddy takes care of me, often inviting me on an afternoon boat ride or down to his cabin for their pre-supper gathering.

Coming to Bear Spring by bus instead of by car is tough, because it doesn't afford me the opportunity to go anywhere in the evening. I suppose I was spoiled by mother all those years when we would have our nightly outings to Waterville. If I'm ever lucky enough to have a vehicle at camp again, I will continue some of the traditions that Mom and I had, and establish new ones of my own. A lot of the people we used to visit are no longer with us, like Aunt Jiggs, but her niece Tally lives in the area and I'm sure she would love having a visit now and then.

It's been many years since I actually played miniature golf. There is still one place in Waterville that has a course. Gifford's Famous Ice Cream, which has miniature golf and batting cages, is where most people hang out in the early evening. Quite a number of years back the miniature golf course got a face lift and is now one of the top golf courses around. Since I no longer partake in the benefit softball game, I just never seem to bother with the old batting cage. Dave and his family do go down for one family outing during their week and I go with them to enjoy the evening.

For those who read my first book about Bear Spring Camps, you know some of the traditions my mother and I had on the road to camp. On the bus, I can't do any of those. First off, I am on the bus company's timetable as to when we stop. I cannot stop for Massachusetts clam chowder or that first Maine lobster roll in a service area off the Maine turnpike. Mom and I never traveled to Maine and back after dark, so we always got to enjoy the beauty of the scenery from Pennsylvania, through New York, and up into New England. The bus travels at night, and I can't view the beauty of the landscape. In the bus depots, layovers can sometimes equal five to six hours, or more. These are extremely tedious for me.

Most of my solitude and thinking time comes right before bed. This past year I had a tape player and some cassettes with me. But the year before that, I would sit in the quiet of the camp with the propane heater going to keep myself toasty warm, and think about all the things that I wished to do that coming year. I have always made good starts to things but hardly ever finished any of them. One year I planned to write a novel; it never happened. I have in very recent years written a play and the first book of camp stories.

Another tradition that I would like to re-instate is the fireside chat interviews on audio tape, like the ones I did with Uncle Cy. Dave and I always talk of making another one but it never seems to happen. Last year he suggested that I interview Ashley or Emily. It is definitely something to keep in mind. I've also thought about asking David to interview me, but I'm not quite sure how that would work out. Perhaps one day we'll give it a go.

I do sadly miss my mom and her friends, who have either passed away or have decided not to come anymore. It was inevitable, but still it hurts. Being in with David's family is wonderful, but as far as me meeting new people … well either I don't have the knack or I'm not trying hard enough. This coming year I'm going to vow to make new friends, to work harder on my own traditions and my own ways of doing things, and to keep myself as independent at camp as possible. Time will tell just how well I accomplish this.

BASKETFUL OF ODD OCCURRENCES TALES

Raccoons Don't Have White Stripes Down Their Backs - During David and my teenage years at Bear Spring Camps, an event took place which taught me to be careful when walking on the grounds of camp at night. It happened at the end of a typical trip to Waterville for ice cream. The time was approximately nine o'clock. During that era at Bear Spring, cars were allowed to park in the open area by the beach. After Dave and I got out of the car, and Mother closed and locked it, all was dark. We, of course, picked that evening to forget our flashlight.

We had planned a Yahtzee tournament for when we all got back, and both Dave and I were eager to get inside to set up the game. In my haste, I did not see the shadowy figure in front of us. Bear Spring has many animals since we are in the heart of nature. With squirrels, raccoons and the occasional moose, it is not uncommon to see something outside at night. Mr. Raccoon sometimes pillages for food from the careless fisherman who leaves his bait outside on the front porch.

All of the sudden, Dave stopped dead in his tracks. He was able to grab my shirt for I was only a step in front of him. "Joey," he whispered, "don't make any sudden movements."

"What's wrong?" I whispered back.

Even Mother, who was weary from the day's activities of fun in the sun and puzzles on the porch, picked up on what David was talking about. As I squinted to see what had caught David's attention, a small animal caught my eye. He was right in our path. "Now, Dave," I said "it's just a raccoon. We have lots of them here."

He replied, "Joey, raccoons don't have white stripes down their backs."

As I always tend to do at the first sign of danger, I overreacted. I yelled, "Skunk!"

David noiselessly put his hand on his forehead as if to say oh brother, now you've done it. Both Mom and Dave were fully expecting the startled skunk to spray. If this had happened that close to our cabin, the three of us would have spent at least one night at the Waterville Holiday Inn; and missed the Bear Spring Camps breakfast, already paid for in the price of the cabin. To our happy amazement, the skunk looked at us, turned away, and waddled off. "Boy you're lucky, Buddy," said David.

Obviously this skunk was looking for his supper. When the critter was out of sight, Mom, David and I slowly made our way up on to the porch and into our cabin. Dave went back outside to make a final check to see if all our bait had been brought in. At $1.50 a dozen for assorted tasty morsels, those delicacies were reserved for the fish, not a skunk.

The next morning there was no sign of the skunk and we never saw him again. Thus ended our only run-in with Mr. White Stripe.

By the Light of the Fiery Moon - When I was in my thirties, my mother and I shared an experience that caught us both off guard. This event took place right after dusk. Mom and I were sitting on our porch and it was a relatively cool evening. We both had on our sweatshirts with long pants, not only to keep us warm but to keep mosquitos from biting. As we were chatting, and enjoying the beginning of our evening, something caught my mother's eye that was so unusual it stopped her mid-sentence.

She pointed off to the horizon behind the cove at Snake Point. As I turned to look, it didn't take me long to see what Mom was noticing. There was a small orange glow on the top of the mountain. It looked like fire. My mother was not the kind of person who panicked easily, and that night was not an exception. She kept a watchful eye on the mountain for several minutes. As sound travels over water, we both listened for sirens, yelling or screaming, or anything that would concretely tell us that something was drastically wrong. We heard nothing.

The glow grew a little taller. I remember Mom saying to me, "That's not right. That's not right at all."

By this time, I think the same thought occurred to us simultaneously. We needed to call the fire department. For some odd reason though, neither one of us moved. Back then, cell phone service was either poor or non-existent at the lake. We would have had to drive up to the main house to make the call on the pay phone. We were not exactly certain where the fire was and did not have an address to give the fire department. We just kept watching, waiting for some sign that someone else had done something. One thing that struck me, as I've thought back on this over the years, was that no one walked over to us, saying something like, "Hey do you see what I see?" Perhaps that is why we didn't act more quickly.

Mother and I were now really in a dilemma as the flames seemed to grow taller with still no signs of any action. We were beginning to wonder if this was some kind of optical illusion, but it couldn't be. Car headlights aren't orange and neither one of us believed this was a UFO. Mom asked me to go inside to get the car keys. The time to act was now. And right then, one of the funniest moments at Bear Spring in my experience took place. The 'fire' lifted off the horizon and was now perched in the sky. "Oh, my God," said my mother. "It's the moon."

Then, in what sounded like a very strange reply, I said, "Are you sure?"

She turned to me and exclaimed, "Fires don't float in the air."

She was absolutely right. Our fireball was now hanging just above the horizon line. It was rather obvious that it was the moon, though neither of us had seen it that orange before. We smiled at one another because we were embarrassed. A short time later, the moon's usual white color was in full force and it was as though nothing had happened.

We were both relieved that nothing was on fire. I'm sure that Mom, although always trying to be on the side of safety, was glad she didn't report the moon coming up to the Oakland or Waterville Fire Department.

Once in a while over the years I have looked for the moon around that same time to see if the phenomenon would repeat itself, and to my recollection it hasn't. Was that such a rare occurrence or have I just missed it?

Mom and I sat on the porch many evenings over the years, talking and joking, and enjoying each other's company. That was truly one of the only evenings, however, that we were glued to an event where all talking ceased and logic went out the window.

Joey Caught a Strange Fish - When I was eleven years old, my mom and I went on a rare mother and son fishing trip. We didn't go far; just past Chutes Channel. We stopped, anchored, and Mom put the worm on my hook. I don't recall whether fishing was brisk or sparse that day but one thing was certain. I caught something that to this day I still remember quite vividly.

We had been there roughly an hour or so when something took my bait. I, of course, got all excited, pulled back to set the hook, and began to reel in. It didn't seem to put up much of a fight, nor did it feel very heavy. I remember thinking to myself that I had probably caught a white or yellow perch. When I finally pulled it up, it shocked both of us.

Mom and I stared at this fish for a moment or two, trying to figure out what it was. It had a tail, was dark green in color, its head looked flattened and the mouth was longer than usual. If I had to describe its head, I would say it had the look of a baby alligator or crocodile, though the rest of it was fish. It was butt-ugly.

For some reason Mom didn't want to touch it. Perhaps she thought it was diseased. So, as I held the fish near the boat, she put on her glove, took some scissors that were in her tackle box, and cut my line. She held it away from herself and quickly dropped the fish back into the lake. I recall asking her what she thought it was. My mother, Dorothy Kockelmans, a Bear Spring Camper for many years, was an avid fisherman. She knew her fish, but had never seen anything like this before.

After fishing another hour or so we decided to head in and talk to Uncle Cy Greco. Surely he would know what it was. To my amazement he was just as dumbfounded as we were. I remember him getting a chuckle out of the fact that Mom wouldn't touch it. "Now, Dorothy, it certainly wasn't going to bite your hand off."

I thought to myself that it was too bad that we didn't have a camera. Armed only with the description, we stopped at various people's camps to see if anyone knew what this hideous looking thing was. From Uncle Cy's cabin, we went next door to the Feldmans who pondered but could not hazard a guess. From there I remember stopping at the Bennetts, who didn't have a clue either. I recall someone, I believe it was Mr. Russell, who said it was possibly a muskellunge, also known as a muskie. He said it was too bad we didn't keep it to show people.

Apparently we were the topic of conversation at supper. People came over to our table offering their suggestions about what our mystery fish might have been. No one seemed to know for certain, not even Bert Mosher. We appreciated everyone's help, but being the talk of the dining hall was a tad embarrassing for us. By the end of suppertime, I was beginning to lose interest in the catch of the day.

Through the years I have thought about what it might have been. The only logical guesses I could come up with were: it was a bass that was genetically mutated, was mangled by a boat's propeller, was attacked by another fish, or was a species of fish that even my mother didn't know about.

In January of this year, Dave finally got the answer. He identified the fish as an Alligator Gar. I looked it up on Yahoo! Images, and found many pictures of the fish that Mom and I pulled out of the lake all those years ago. There was no doubt in my mind that that ugly fish that I caught that day was indeed an Alligator Gar.

The Strange Orange Light – In 2011, during a bonfire at the fire pit near my cabin, I experienced one of the oddest events I have ever seen at Bear Spring. Before the evening was over, I, as well as several others, would see something that we could not explain.

I had invited Dave and all the crew from his family down to my cabin for the evening bonfire. Having always been invited to other people's camps, I figured it was my turn to host the evening event.

It was a moon-lit night. Many people showed up and I was thrilled. We had roughly twenty people there. They brought their own chairs from their cabins and sat in a circle around the pit. Most people brought their own beverages, though I had soda in my fridge in case anyone wanted one. Steve Harvey brought his iPod and plugged it into speakers so we could all enjoy some tunes. The evening started like any other, with good conversation, music, lots of laughs, and stories.

A couple of hours into the festivities, I just happened to look up into the night sky and saw something odd. It was an orange light high in the sky. Oh, my goodness, was I finally seeing my first UFO?

Whatever this thing was, it captured the attention of many others. Cell phone cameras quickly popped out of people's pockets. The music went off and several of us walked close to my dock, so as to be able to get a better look at the object.

We all watched this thing for several minutes. Now I know my aircraft, and even from high distances on a clear night, I can usually see the red and green flashing wing lights. I saw nothing but an orange light moving slowly toward us. The object seemed to slow down and no one heard any noise. A few people got excited while others became a bit concerned. I was one of the concerned folks. Even though I wasn't afraid, take me to your leader was not in my evening plans.

The object appeared to come to a stop before turning out toward Otter Island. Several minutes later it disappeared into some clouds and was not seen again. Dave thought it might have been a fighter jet. He might have been correct, but I would have thought a fighter jet would have made noise. Perhaps it was too high up to hear. The one thing that truly fascinated me was its apparent lack of speed. Before it made its turn out toward Otter Island, it almost seemed to stop. No airplane that I know of can do that. If it was a helicopter, which can hover, I would have expected to hear the swishing of the rotors.

After the bonfire was over, I sat inside my cabin, straining my brain thinking about what it might have been. I thought to myself, certainly we'll see something about it in the morning paper. We never did. That lends credence to David's suggestion that perhaps it was an army aircraft.

After breakfast, not many spoke of the orange light and the topic died out. For the briefest of moments, however, I was sure that I would see in the morning headlines, "UFO spotted over North Bay." Just like the evening when my mother and I saw the orange moon come over the mountain top, believing it was fire, I am most glad I didn't contact anyone saying, hey, I just saw a UFO.

RUN-AWAY BOAT

It was a hot early August day, and David and I decided to enjoy our daily afternoon boat ride. We usually took the *Galileo,* of which I was always the captain, but on this particular occasion we decided to take the small camp boat so that Dave could take the helm. He called his boat the *Spidinkies.* He got that name from a family member who used that word instead of cussing.

We made one complete lap around North Bay, which in the smaller boat took twice as long as in the *Galileo*. Dave asked me if I wanted to go around again. I said sure, why not? It was a beautiful day, we had plenty of gas, and nothing else was planned for that afternoon. Dave began the second lap.

Then it happened.

I do not know what possessed me to do this, but I, a crazy young teenager, dared the driver to jump out of the boat. David told me later that he yelled up to me not to dare him because he would do it, but I didn't hear him. I yelled back again, making sure that my voice was heard over the engine, "Dave, I triple double dog dare you to jump out of this boat." Figuring that sanity and his sense of well-being would override temptation, the thought never entered my mind that he would actually take me up on the dare.

I heard nothing in reply and for a few moments the *Spidinkies* turned as it should have to avoid markers and other boats.

We passed Snake Point and began running parallel to the lakefront, within sight of the cabins. There was a platform anchored about thirty yards from shore that people used for diving and lying in the sun. We were approximately eighty to one hundred yards away when I noticed three beautiful teenage girls, about fifteen or sixteen years old, sunbathing. Unless we turned quickly, the boat would hit the platform and the girls.

"Ok, Dave, nice, slow, easy turn."

Nothing happened. Well maybe he just didn't hear me.

"Ok, Dave, nice slow …"

Then horror hit me. Could it be that this slightly older, slightly wiser person took the dare? I realized I had to look back. To my shock I was in a run-away boat. Dave was treading water with one hand while waving to me with the other about fifty yards back. Blind panic set in. I jumped over two bench seats - carefully - to get to the engine.

I had two options. Option number one was to turn the boat to the left away from shore, which would have thrown me off balance and caused me to go into the drink as well. Option number two, and the one I chose, was to put the engine from forward into reverse without pausing in neutral. The engine whined with resistance and the propeller broke the waterline for an instant. I felt like the captain of the *Titanic* praying that he didn't hit the iceberg. All three girls dove off into the water, swimming toward safety. Dave told me later that he had reduced the speed and thought I knew he was jumping out. He assumed I would have plenty of time to take control of the boat. To me, it felt like the boat was going full-speed and that it took forever for my thirteen year-old badly balanced body to avoid disaster. The boat stopped mere feet from the diving platform before slowly reversing.

After I had gotten the boat under my control, I looked back at Dave. His coy smile had long since gone from his face. I went back to him, the engine sputtering, not running smoothly at all. When I got to him, I shouted over the engine's noise, "Do you think that was funny, mister?"

Now to this day I do not recall his reply verbatim; I think I was too angry. But suffice it to say that since he left me in the lurch, I would leave him. I drove away, leaving him to swim to shore. Granted it wasn't that far of a swim. Little did I know that he would get the last laugh.

While all this was going on, I failed to notice that my mother was sitting on the porch and saw the whole thing. As I docked the boat, she came out to greet me. "Why did David jump out of that boat?" she said. And I, the naïve truth telling idiot that I was, offered up, "Because I dared him to."

Mother couldn't believe what she just heard. Oh, she was proud of her son for telling the truth, but not for being so irresponsible as to dare the driver of a moving object to jump out. Moments later David arrived on shore. He has a knack of sneaking up on me if he wants to. Oh, yes, he was going to have his revenge for being left behind. And my mother, God rest her saintly soul, never let on that he was standing directly behind me.

"But Mom," I explained, "I didn't think he would really do it."

I kind of had a sense that my buddy and brother was behind me. I can just feel those kinds of things. I slowly turned my head around to see him grinning at me. I stood there, Mother to my front, David at my rear, trying to figure out how I was going to get out of this predicament. The way I had it figured was that I had two people upset with me. After several minutes of explanation, squirming, and perspiring, Mother looked at David and said, "So he dared you, huh?"

He shook his head in the affirmative with a big grin on his face. Right there I knew I'd had it. Dave looked up at her and said, "Mom, can I dunk him?"

She waited for an agonizing second before saying, "Sure, why not?"

I tried to flee. I took a step and a half before I felt David's arms around my waist. "Where do you think you're going, Kockelmans?" he joked.

I could always tell when David was not really mad at me. Yet my leaving him in the lake did require a good dunking. And at the count of three, that was exactly what I got. Into the shallow water I went with a kersplash. Luckily, I was in my bathing suit so it didn't matter.

"Ok," I said, "fair is fair. Dave, remind me never to dare you to jump out of the boat again."

"Joe, never dare me to jump out of the boat."

"I hate it when you do that."

The next morning, unfortunately, we had to have the engine looked at by one of the cabin boys. He popped off the top to give it a good once over. To my relief, the damage was minimal. The engine was not ruined.

That ended my daring days. Any such further dares of my friend David occurred on dry land.

BASKETFUL OF ON THE LAKE TALES

The Morning of the Eagle - 2009 was the first year I rode up to Maine and back home in a Greyhound bus. Doing so, of course, I was on their timetable. For my return trip, I had to wait until mid-afternoon, 2:30 if memory serves, to be at the bus depot. This afforded me an opportunity to leisurely pack up, officially check out of my cabin by 10 a.m., and stay on the camp grounds for a few extra hours. Though I had to pay for it, I actually got to enjoy a second delicious Saturday dinner.

Before we went up to that noon meal, a few of my friends decided they were going to take a boat ride in one of the camp boats. They asked me if I wanted to go along. I, always loving boats and the lake, didn't have to be asked twice.

Four of us went along that day: Amanda and Jeremy Lindstrom, Amanda's sister Leah Harvey, and me. The weather could not have been better. All the rest of my clothes were packed and I was forced to wear my hoodie. Once out there I was quite warm. I wished I had a t-shirt under my hoodie, so that I could have taken the outer layer off. But the breeze, when the boat was moving, made it quite bearable.

Jeremy remarked that Dave had mentioned that there was once a bald eagle's nest high atop the pine trees of Snake Point. We decided to go to see if we could locate them. Amanda had a digital camera and we were hoping to get some really good shots. First we had to find the birds.

When we arrived at the mouth of the cove by Snake Point, I vaguely remembered where David had pointed them out to me. They were nesting in one of the tallest trees, about nine or ten in from Snake Point. We looked and looked, but to our disappointment no one could find them. I got the idea to slowly go around to the other side to see if we could spot them from there. We went around Snake Point into North Bay.

We were almost ready to pull away when Jeremy finally spotted one of them. I remember Amanda trying to get a quick picture, but it looked like a little white dot on her digital camera screen. We were either too far away or the eagle was too hidden in the foliage.

I knew that there would be a much better vantage point from where we were originally. So carefully and quietly we doubled back until we spotted them. Mr. and Mrs. Eagle were snuggled in their nest, one of them keeping a sharp eye on us. Amanda very carefully began taking pictures. With the sun as bright as it was that day, I remember her remarking that she was having trouble seeing through the view finder, and was not certain if she was getting good shots. Later on back at the Harvey cabin's porch, we deemed them to be excellent, better than we could have imagined.

After about ten to twelve minutes of bird watching and picture taking, Jeremy saw that I was getting a tad uncomfortable in my sweatshirt. He said, "Hey, why don't we go for a nice long ride to cool us off?" I was thrilled.

We began slowly, so as not to startle the birds, but once past Snake Point we headed back into North Bay and Jeremy opened the throttle to full. Even though the camp boats were much slower than the *Galileo* was, any breeze was most welcomed. It truly was an exceptional ending to a great week. I was feeling a bit sad for I knew once we got back to shore, and finished eating dinner, it would soon be time for Dan Harvey to take me into Waterville to the bus.

Some of those photographs were placed on my Facebook page and remain there to this day as a nice reminder of that last boat ride of '09.

Special Fishing Hook Nooks - As fishermen on Great Pond for many years, David and I, along with Uncle Cy Greco, tended to stay on our side of the lake. That consisted of North Bay, Snake Point and its cove, along with Otter and Oak Islands.

Great Pond is nine miles long, and is four and a half miles at its widest point. It has many nooks and crannies, shoals, and coves, which provide a plethora of wonderful fishing spots. Once a year my boat mates and I, and sometimes Bob Smarz, would venture to the other end of the lake for a special day of fishing. Three places I enjoyed going to were the Salmon Hole, Pinkham's Cove, and Austin Bog.

At sixty feet deep, the Salmon Hole is one of the deepest parts of Great Pond. Uncle Cy, Dave, and I always tried to come down from breakfast and be ready to leave as soon as we could to enjoy maximum fishing time after travel. Extra anchor rope would be obtained from the cabin boy just in case it would be needed. This trip would only be taken on what my mother referred to as a good lake day, meaning sunny skies and calm lake conditions. With the speed of the *Galileo* we would be able to get there within fifteen minutes; much sooner than if we would have taken a camp boat.

Once at the Salmon Hole, either Dave or Uncle Cy would attach the extra rope to the *Galileo's* anchor apparatus. The actual hole was not a very large area. I once looked at a map of the entire lake, verifying that the water level around that area was indeed less deep. Staying in one spot was the key. I always knew that Uncle Cy had hit the mark correctly when he would turn to us, smile, and say, "Salmon beware."

With our usual assortment of bait, including worms, frogs, hellgrammites and crayfish, denizens of the deep would have a wide assortment of food. Little did they know that their brunch would have a hook attached to it. Sometimes the Salmon Hole would be a crap shoot. We could sit for two or three hours and not get a nibble. On hotter days the fish would be down deeper and would be harder to catch. Or we could get nice sized bass or salmon, pickerel or trout. One time Mr. Greco caught a beautiful, long pickerel and decided to give it to Mr. Deacon, a long time Bear Spring camper who just loved to eat them.

As for me, I don't recall getting anything of size there; perhaps a nice white perch or a medium sized bass. Uncle Cy and David, as they usually did, seemed to have the luck; catching much better fish than I.

We usually only went to Pinkham's Cove once per year. It was our special treat. It would take twelve to fifteen minutes to travel there over water. I remember it not being especially deep there, though the fishing was quite excellent. White perch of good size and hefty bass were waiting to be caught by anglers.

Uncle Cy caught a very nice eighteen inch bass there once. He knew to always keep his rod tip down to prevent the big ones from breaking water and possibly spitting the hook. Generally, the larger the bass the less of a fight they put up. The smaller bass are most certainly the feistier ones. This particular day, Cy had what he always called 'a goodie.' It was our practice that when someone got a big fish someone would help to net it; because of my left side weakness, due to Cerebral Palsy, it was Dave who would net Cy's bigger fish. I didn't want to run the risk of losing the big one and/or falling in.

Pinkham's Cove had many pretty houses lining its shore. Quite a few had boat houses, which led me to believe that they were year round homes, and that the boats would be pulled out of the water to be stored for the winter.

Dave and I stopped going to Pinkham's in the mid to late 90s when we learned that fish in the cove were diseased with worms. We were heartily disappointed when we found out about the sickly fish. Sure, we all could have simply caught and released, but the idea of handling a diseased fish did not appeal to me. Also, Uncle Cy did not want to waste time and gas for fish he couldn't keep. The worm problem could not be fixed, according to what I was told. It's a shame, for I always found it challenging fishing.

On the other side of Great Pond was Austin Bog. Austin Bog was never one of our fishing spots. It was just a place to look at scenery, see if there were any frogs on the lily pads, and take a glimpse at my favorite thing to look at, the old pink boathouse. It looked like it could fall over any minute, yet it stood for years.

On numerous occasions, Dave and I would putt slowly and carefully as close as we dared, looking for a house on the land nearby. All I ever saw were trees. Whose boathouse that was, I will never know. Once, with David sitting beside me, I piloted the *Galileo* to the opening of the boathouse. The water was deep enough to go in, but when I peered inside I saw just how rickety it was and decided not to push my luck. While the boat was in reverse, I looked at Dave. He looked thoroughly relieved. The last time I went there to see it was in 2002, and it was still standing. In 2011, I learned that the boathouse did indeed collapse a few years back.

The trips to the other end of the lake would not be attempted on rough weather days, as I mentioned before. With the sixty horse-power engine and choppy conditions, a miserable ride was all but guaranteed. When we would all go to the Salmon Hole, Pinkham's Cove, or Austin Bog, we would go after breakfast on a sunny day, when the water was as calm as glass. I could open up the throttle and get us there quickly.

While we were on our way, though I was paying attention to driving the boat, sometimes I would let my mind wander a bit to the fishing trip that happened the day before, the bonfire we took part in, or sometimes even thoughts of what I would do the coming year.

The last few years that I had the *Galileo* we stuck more to North Bay, the cove off Snake Point, and on the back side of Otter Island. To this day I still fish, but I do so in a boat rented by one of Dave's brothers-in-law, hence, I go where they take me. And so far that has not been to the Salmon Hole, Pinkham's Cove, or Austin Bog.

Going Down the Runway - The worst mishap the *Galileo* ever endured was due to lack of planning. It was a hot breezy afternoon. David, Pop, and I decided to cool ourselves down with a long boat ride. Mom decided to stay behind on the porch with a cool drink. We were going to go to the other side of Great Pond where any breeze might be stronger. It was an area that none of us went to very often. After we got back, I wished that I had, the night before, asked Mr. Mosher for a lake map that I could study before we left. But I didn't.

The ride started out in North Bay as usual. We then started making our way through Chutes Channel to the other side. We were enjoying our ride with the *Galileo's* throttle open to full. She was getting a good workout. On this rare occasion, I was not at the helm. Dave had taken a turn driving and then Pop took his turn; a rarity for

Dad. I should have been paying attention to his driving so that I could assist him as needed, but I didn't think of it.

It was during Pop's turn at the wheel when the minor tragedy occurred. We were on our way back to North Bay (where we knew what the markers meant) but we were unsure of the markers on the other side. He had to navigate the *Galileo* in an area where rocks were abundant. On one side was a row of green markers and on the other side, approximately ten yards away on the left, was a row of red markers. Pop must have thought that in between the rows of markers was the danger zone. As it turns out, it was the safe passage. Just like landing an aircraft, we should have aimed right down the middle of the runway. Pop veered to the right toward the rocks.

By this point in the ride, I was sitting in the front passenger area half asleep. I got a rude awakening. As the propeller smacked against a boulder just underneath the water surface, the *Galileo* come out of the water for a fraction of a second. Pop immediately brought the boat to a halt. As he lifted the engine up with the automatic lifting device, he asked, "Davey, do you see any damage?"

Dave, though not really wanting to be the bearer of bad news, replied, "Um, yes, sir, there is."

I quickly walked back to where the engine was. Luckily the boat itself was undamaged. To this day, I don't know how the propeller was the only thing that hit the rock, but it happened. With the propeller in the mangled shape it was in, we weren't getting out of that spot on our own. I reached into the glove box, got the air horn, and blew it to call for help. After several minutes, someone came to our aid and carefully got us out of the rocky situation we were in.

Once back in deep water, the ride home was slow but uneventful. The propeller was just useable enough for us to drive our boat back to our dock at the slowest possible speed, although the engine put out a rough quiver. I kept thinking to myself, now how am I going to explain this to Mother? Pop assured me that he would take full responsibility. I felt guilty, yet relieved.

That evening, Mother went up to supper early to place a call to the marina right before it closed. A mechanic was up the next morning to not only install the new propeller but to inspect the engine for any other damage. To my relief, when the new propeller was put on, everything else checked out ok. Mom told all of us that she would greatly appreciate it if we would stay on our side of the lake.

The next morning, Uncle Cy, David, and I planned and partook of a fishing trip. The engine started up as usual and ran smoothly. I purposely opened her up to full throttle to check for any vibration. Thankfully, it was as though the entire incident never happened.

A month or so later, when the marina bill was sent to our home in Pennsylvania, Mom showed me how much the new propeller cost. I felt like crawling under the rock that we had hit.

Off to Find the Loons - In 1987, Pop, David, and I set out in the *Galileo* to find some loons. We had my Panasonic camcorder in hand and I knew of several places that the birds might be found. It was a rare boat ride for my dad. I'm not trying to say that my father didn't like the *Galileo,* but I think he liked sitting on the porch with Mom, listening to his classical music, or wading into the lake on his personal float much better. When he heard that we were going to try to take home movies of the loons, however, he seemed eager to go with us.

Today, the loons are more used to people and can sometimes be found right in North Bay near Bear Spring Camps. Not so years ago. Campers would usually have to go past Oak Island or perhaps even to the other side of the lake to spot the birds.

The first place we looked was behind Otter Island. This small uninhabited piece of land was clearly visible from camp. From there we headed to the back of Oak Island. That is where David spotted a loon. I was driving, Pop was co-pilot, and Dave, with his steadier hand, was cameraperson. Dad warned me not to get too close and he was quite correct; they startle very easily.

I switched off the engine so as not to make as much noise. We were too far away on our first attempt to see the loon clearly. Even with the zoom on the camera, Dave could not get a good shot. You could see the bird but not the fine details that we wanted. Dave whispered to me, "Why don't you try moving in just a little closer at slow speed."

As I started the engine, the bird looked over at us. I was hoping he wouldn't dive under the water, for he could re-appear almost anywhere. Loons are fast swimmers under water. All the sudden, out of the corner of my eye, I spotted a second loon. It was watching us intensely as it joined its partner. They began to call back and forth to one another. I'd have given my left arm to understand what they were saying. I kept looking for a little baby, which would have been on one of their backs. But no such luck.

Looking back on it now, they looked like a couple to me. So we'll refer to them as Larry and Lucy.

Dave asked me to slowly spiral around the birds so as not to startle them. It took *forever,* as the orbits got tighter and tighter toward them, but eventually we got some awesome footage. When we got back to camp and popped the VHS into the small combo TV/VCR player, we were amazed at the vivid colors of the birds. Also many of the loon calls were captured on the tape, which was something I had always wanted to have.

The next afternoon, we again set out to search for our loons. There they were behind Oak, looking at us as if to say, well it certainly took you long enough to come back.

To my surprise, they let us get closer to them more easily. Dave, a bird expert, called to them and one of them answered him. Dad attempted to make a loon call, but couldn't do it quite as well as David did. It gave us all a chuckle.

We very carefully lowered the anchor and sat with our new friends for a good thirty minutes. They, over time, inched closer to us and got within I'd say twenty yards of the *Galileo.* Dave took some more video footage and a few still pictures.

When we arrived back on the third day, Larry and Lucy were not there. We searched for them a bit, in the various small coves in the area, with no luck. Perhaps they flew off to visit another of the Belgrade Lakes.

I still have what I now call the loon video. Every time I watch it, it takes me back to those special few days. Even though I don't watch my Maine videos as much as I used to, occasionally I will dig up the lake tapes, the video fireside chat with Uncle Cy Greco, and most of all, the video of our friends Larry and Lucy the loons.

GAME NIGHT, ANYONE?

One evening a number of years back, Dave, a couple of his nephews, and a brother-in-law were going to get together to have an evening of poker for penny-ante stakes. Now, I am not a gambler. As a matter of fact I don't particularly like cards. Dave knew I wanted to fit into the family more, so he suggested that I come over and join the game. "It will be fun," he said. "And just watch, you'll be the big winner. Just watch." It didn't take much arm twisting, for even if I lost my shirt in the game I'd be having fun with Dave and family. To me, that is the main reason why I go to camp. I love my family and friends.

The game was to begin at eight o'clock. That gave Dave and me a chance to sneak out for the briefest of evening fishing trips nearby in North Bay. I remember vividly as we fished, Dave explained the rules of the various games. Herein lies one of my problems. With short-term memory being affected by Cerebral Palsy, people can explain things to me in the simplest of fashions, yet sometimes it takes a couple of go 'rounds until I fully comprehend it. This is what was happening during this fishing excursion. Try as he might, without any cards in front of me to look at, I just couldn't grasp all the rules.

He told me not to worry and explained that before the game started we would go over things one more time.

"Won't that take up actual game time?" I asked.

Dave assured me that no one would mind taking a few extra moments at the beginning of the evening to make sure that a player knew what he was doing. 7:15 rolled around and Dave and I headed the *Galileo* back to my dock. We had some extra time to relax because the game was just next door in the Merkhofer cabin.

I remember bringing a two-liter bottle of soda of one type or another while others brought chips, pretzels, and beer. It certainly looked like someone had bought out a small grocery store; enough munchies and beverages to last many hours. I pulled up a seat in front of the old coffee table. I had my jar of pennies in hand. Dave and his brother-in-law Ray very quickly explained the rules once again. Dave said, "Don't worry, Joe, if you have any questions just ask." And, with a smile on his face, informed me that if I were the big winner I would be used as bait the next morning. Of course I knew he was kidding.

Ray said the first game was five card draw ... or five card stud ... or five card something. I tossed my penny in the middle of the table and the cards were dealt. I had an uneasy feeling that I still had no idea what I was doing. I had two tens in my hand. When it came my turn to tell the dealer how many new cards I wanted, with only the knowledge of what a good card hand is from playing Yahtzee, I asked for three cards. I saw David's slight smile when I gave away more than half my hand. I did not possess a good poker face. If I had received the other two tens and a king, I probably would have had difficulty concealing my enthusiasm.

When all the cards had been dealt and it was time to find out who won, somehow my two tens held up. I had won the first game. I often wondered if Dave and the crew let me win. He claimed not. As the evening went on, I held my own, not making big returns but not losing my shirt either. Soon it became the running gag that when it was my turn to deal, I chose five card draw. It was the game I knew the best and the game with which I had won the most.

The time came around 9:30 to take our first stretch and cigarette break. Dave wanted to see me on the porch. I thought I was in trouble. "Where'd you learn to play cards, Kockelmans?" he said smiling.

"I don't really know what I'm doing," I replied. "I'm just kind of doing what everyone else is doing."

Dave made mention that he had been keeping track and that I was slightly ahead in my winnings. He, of course, couldn't be happier for me. These games, just like Yahtzee tournaments, are more for fun than anything else.

About fifteen minutes later we began playing again. It was once again my turn to deal and choose the game. Now, I had been listening to what other people had been saying during the evening, such as which cards were wild, if there were certain rules, etc. I decided to get cute. I said, "Let's do five card draw, aces, deuces and tens are wild." Laughter filled the room. In unison both Dave and Ray said no, no, only one wild card per game. With my low self-esteem problem, had it been anyone other than family, I would have wanted to hide under the table. I went back to my old standby, five card draw and chose aces wild.

During the second half of the game, Dave's nephews started to have all the luck. Dave, Ray, and I would win occasionally, but the younger bunch began to win more often. Only playing for pennies, no one was going to get rich. But as the evening wore on, the game did seem to take a slightly more serious tone. There was less joking around and more intensity. That was fine with me, I don't mind good competition. As the hour drew nearer to 11:00, I was so fatigued that I was starting to lose my concentration. With Dave and me going fishing in the morning, it was almost my bedtime anyway. I patiently waited until it was time for me to deal again before using the old card expression, "Deal me out."

I learned from Dave the next morning that the game didn't last much longer after I left. He asked me if I had enjoyed myself and I told him that I had quite a blast. Everybody was happy that I took part in the evening and was glad that I had so much fun. I only recall ever playing cards with them one other time, but that is probably just due to the fact that cards aren't my game.

Other activities that Dave, his family, and I have enjoyed are Wiffle ball, beach volley ball, and a tennis ball toss in the lake. I certainly did enjoy each one of those as well, but I have fond memories of that first card game. It made me feel like I truly was part of the family.

***

My best friend Dave and I, especially in the 1980s, loved to play Yahtzee when we would return from evening trips to Waterville. We would usually challenge ourselves to a best two out of three. This usually took about an hour and a half. Sometimes Mom would join in. When she did that, Dave and I put our competition aside and we would just play until we got tired.

Dave ended up winning most of the games. Occasionally I would get the extra Yahtzee or what I would call the Up-Top bonus and squeak out a victory. Even though Dave raised his eyebrow in displeasure, I knew he was just kidding and was happy when I won. My buddy gets competitive sometimes as do I. Whether it be in Wiffle ball, football, or a Yahtzee tournament, we both have that competitive edge.

I can remember games when Dave would start out rolling a Yahtzee his first turn. I would say, whoops, I lost. Of course we would play out the game. Another time I remember getting my 3 of kind, 4 of kind, and Yahtzee on my first three turns while David struggled with his 1s, 2s, and 3s. Luck usually shined with my buddy, and even when he was behind, he would get a Yahtzee or a 4 of a kind, and end up winning those games anyway.

One year, there was a version of the game called Triple Yahtzee. I thought to myself, oh, boy, here's one evening's match in one neat package. It was three games at the same time. However, when we played all three games in one, it was a jumbled mess. It was harder to get everything without getting zeros. There was also a version we saw at K-Mart called Word Yahtzee. As I recall, it didn't last long. To me, Yahtzee is numbers.

Now that Dave is married, our Yahtzee days are long over. His evenings are filled with his family's activities. I tend to keep to myself after dark, except for attending an occasional bonfire.

As I recall, Dave's daughters or other family members never joined us for a Yahtzee game, but I could be wrong, it's been so many years. Tournaments and championships come and go, mini-golf winners are crowned and forgotten, the fishing contest winner is crowned from one year to the next, but those fond memories of the early years of Yahtzee will remain vivid in my mind.

***

In the late 1990s, for at least three years, my friends Rick Bennett, Sam Dunn, and I would take part in a board game called *Star Wars* Trivial Pursuit. We would select an evening and the combatants would gather at my mom's cabin for the special contest. Sue Smarz read the questions from the cards, so that we could concentrate on our answers. One year Erin McCue was there with us and took turns reading with Sue.

Despite it being a friendly game, there was intense competition when we got together for those couple of hours after supper. So intense in fact that when we were asked a question for a wedge piece, answers had to match what was on the card exactly. The game was based on the original *Star Wars* movies, *A New Hope, The Empire Strikes Back,* and *Return of the Jedi*, episodes IV, V, and VI. Rick Bennett was the master of this game. Most times he would be able to answer the question before it was finished. He was the champion every year we played.

Usually Sam and I would battle for second place. The game could be played with up to four players and if memory serves, Mike Comick played with us one or two years. Though it was obviously all in fun, I wish that at least one time I would have been able to defeat Rick.

The way the game worked was quite cool. It had a standard Trivial Pursuit game board, but instead of a die, there was a miniature R2D2. When you pushed its dome, a randomized number came up on the front LED display. R2 also came complete with sound effects: squeaks, whistles and bleeps.

Why our championship didn't last more than a few years I cannot recall, but I do remember that at some point the droid dice-roller began malfunctioning, due to age and wear and tear. Back home I would play this game with a friend of mine, Jim Sneeringer, every Thursday night. That's basically what drove me nuts. The game was mine, I practiced all year, and still I could not defeat Rick Bennett.

Today no championships are held; no board games, no miniature golf, no fishing contests. Rick is busy with his family, which I know he loves. The only time I see Sam Dunn now, is up at the dining hall. Sometimes I chat with him on the porch of the main house while he is on his laptop. And since I have gotten back to camp, I hang out with the Trost family. It's funny how even at Bear Spring, where things seem not to change, they do.

BASKETFUL OF FAMILY AND FRIENDS TALES

Where Oh Where Has My Little Sister Gone? - In 2002, I had the opportunity to see family bonds at work. It was a truly gratifying experience. On a dim, misty early evening, I had just returned from supper. I had sat down on one of the porch chairs for a few minutes of quiet contemplation before going inside the cabin for the night. Mom and I were not planning to go anywhere, as I remember. We had made plans to play some Yahtzee, before finishing the evening watching a video tape of *Yanni Live at the Acropolis*.

David and I consider ourselves brothers, and when he got married to Geri, who he met at camp, I became uncle to his nieces and nephews. When he and his wife had children, I was their uncle as well. He had married into a large family who had been going to Bear Spring Camps for many years. The Harvey and Merkhofer kids took to me right away, but the Moran children were a little slower to warm up to me.

I was just about ready to go inside when I noticed my niece, Sonia Moran, around eight years old at the time, walking toward me. I could tell that something wasn't quite right. She looked sad and worried. Once she spotted me, she picked up her pace. In a very shy voice, she asked me whether or not I could help her. Of course the answer was yes.

"What's wrong?" I asked.

"I've lost my little sister. Can you help me find her?"

I was only too happy to oblige.

Mind you, Bear Spring Camps is quite safe. It's not like the big city with its traffic or crime. But still, little children should not walk around unattended.

Walking away from Mom's cabin toward the bridge, I reached out my right hand in a show of strength and support. With Sonia being new to the "Uncle Joey as part of the family" concept, I wasn't sure if she was going to take my hand or not. When she did, it showed me that she'd put her trust in me. I was not going to let her down.

First we arrived back at her cabin and checked all the rooms carefully. Then we checked the Trost cabin to see if Corri was playing with her cousins, Ashley and Emily. No such luck; the cabin was empty. Next we checked the back road to see if Corri had gone for a walk. When we got to the end of the lane at the property's edge without sight of her, or other nieces and nephews, we decided to double back. It was time to see if Corri had returned to the main house.

Somehow I got the idea that Sonia was scared to go into the dining room. If Corri was not there, we would have been out of places to look. She then would have had to tell her mother that she had lost track of her little sister. I told Sonia that I would walk in first and look toward their table to see if Corri was there. To my happy surprise, she was sitting on her mommy's lap. To me it didn't matter what had transpired or exactly how she had gotten there, I was just glad she was safe and sound. Sonia was also quite relieved to see her.

The next morning I asked Sonia what had happened. She told me that Corri went looking for their mother. Not finding her in the cabin, she decided to check the dining hall. She probably should have taken Sonia with her, but at her age wanting mommy was a more powerful force at that particular moment than anything else.

David's Rude Awakening - In the late 1970s, a trip back home from Waterville one evening had an unexpected moment. The evening started as any other at camp. Mom, David and I had a delicious supper and went to Rummel's for ice cream and miniature golf later that evening. We left camp at approximately 8:00. The ride lasted fifteen minutes. Both David and I were wide awake and eager with anticipation for our ice cream.

There was usually a line of customers at the serving windows. There were many camps in that area, as well as local people who were regular patrons. Mom asked David and me to have our order in mind so that we would not keep people behind us waiting too long.

My choice was easy. Coffee ice cream if they had it, vanilla if they didn't. I believe Dave chose black cherry.

After ice cream, it was time to have a fun game of miniature golf. Yes, we both liked to win at the things we did, but as anyone who has played the game can attest to, miniature golf is $1/10^{th}$ skill and $9/10^{th}$ luck.

On the average, Dave would usually defeat me by ten to fifteen strokes. As I can recall, I don't think I ever beat him in miniature golf; certainly not during the championship years when Uncle Cy Greco joined us. Mom never played. Whether she didn't like miniature golf or didn't want to expend the energy, we will never know. Usually she would sit in the car with the windows down while she listened to music. Rummel's almost always had WGAN-FM playing on their outdoor speakers. Every time our song, "Theme from *A Summer Place*," began to play, our game of golf came to a screeching halt. "No, no," I said to David, "I have to hear this song." The only times he ever put up an opposition was when there were people behind us and he didn't want us to hold them up. He would either insist we keep playing or tell the folks behind us that they could go ahead and play through.

If the benefit softball game had not taken place yet, and we still had enough energy, Dave and I would take twenty swings each in the batting cage. Once ice cream and all activities were done, it was time to head back to camp. This would usually be between 9:30 and 10:00. After listening to soft soothing music playing on the speakers, expending energy trying to make all our golf shots count, and a fifteen minute car ride at the end, either Dave or I would become sleepy and doze off on the way back. This particular evening it was David who dozed.

I remember the event distinctly. Mom was driving and I was in the front passenger seat of the old Cadillac. Dave was sprawled out on the back seat. After a few minutes, I remember asking him a question and not getting an answer. Mom checked the rear view mirror, smiled, and whispered to me, "He's fast asleep."

As we drove through the countryside with the car radio playing, I too found it hard to keep my eyes open. We were almost back to camp when it happened. Mom exclaimed, "Watch out," as she hit the brakes. I remember two things. First, seeing Mr. and Mrs. Raccoon with their little raccoons behind them crossing the road, and second, my buddy Dave saying a few choice words before his body rolled off onto the floorboard. Mom and I asked him if he was ok. I looked back to see him give us the old hand wave as he said, "Thank goodness I wasn't eating ice cream at the time. I'd have been wearing it."

I told him that we were doing our best to not have massive raccoon road kill. He was happy to hear that the animal family was freaked out but unharmed. Mom in a semi-joking manner said to Dave, "That's why I always get the car checked out before leaving for Maine. I always tell the mechanic to make sure my brakes are in top working order."

We were only two hundred yards or so from the Bear Spring Camps turnoff. As the raccoons faded off into the darkness, we continued, got back to camp safely, locked up the car, and went inside. As I recall, we weren't up that much longer. With a big fishing trip planned for the morning, Dave and I turned in, none the worse for wear.

Seeing Double - In the late 1970s, I had an unusual experience with two very pretty girls. Twin sisters. I know up until now I have used real names, but I think in this story I shall change their names for privacy reasons. We shall refer to them as Betsy and Beth.

It has been my experience that identical twins, especially when they are children, are extremely difficult to tell apart. As it turned out, I would be tested before the vacation would be over, and I would fail miserably. I have thought about this a lot over the years and wished that I had done a few things differently.

When I first met the twins, Betsy was a little more outgoing than her sister. I, around the age of thirteen and just becoming interested in girls, was looking for that first love. After a couple of days of talking to one another and enjoying each other's company, our eyes locked during a conversation by the fireplace. We both leaned in for a kiss and I must say it was magical …as magical for a thirteen year old as it could be.

As for Beth, the other twin, she and I were friends and the three of us enjoyed outdoor activities together. There didn't seem to be any jealousy on her part. After about a week, however, of seeing her identical twin sister having her hand held, her lips kissed, and being hugged, jealousy began to rear its ugly head.

As I recall, Betsy usually wore a certain kind of top, much more girly if you would, with lace and ruffles. Beth usually wore something more plain. As for their hair, no help there in telling them apart. One day Beth had an opportunity to test me. Sadly enough I failed miserably. To this day I'm not sure where Betsy was, but Beth put on one of her sister's tops and a pair of blue jeans, came over and knocked on our cabin door. Whether she had overheard Betsy and me talking about things we liked, or perhaps plans for the rest of the day, she had a good idea that I'd be at my cabin. She pretended to be her sister. What a thorough job she did, too. I fell for the trap hook line and sinker. Immediately after kissing her, I knew something didn't feel right, but I couldn't put my finger on it. This is where I made the mistake I regret. After spending so much time with Betsy, I should have known the difference with Beth, but I didn't. I really thought I was smooching with my girlfriend.

After sitting and talking for a while longer, she went back to her cabin. To my surprise, a few minutes later, an angry Betsy came over. I asked, what's wrong, I thought we just had a perfectly wonderful time. She said, you did, with my sister. I had been had.

After speaking with Betsy, it dawned on us that her sister had played a trick on the both of us. We weren't amused. After confronting Beth, she confessed, and as I recall she looked ashamed of herself. I asked her why she did it. And in front of her sister and me, she gave a completely honest answer. She wanted me for herself. She looked just like her sister, and yet I hadn't chosen her. I felt like a heel.

Oddly enough, the next year it was Beth who sparked my interest and we had our little fling. Betsy told me that during the school year she got a boyfriend and was no longer available.

Beth and I had a lovely two weeks together. We did many of the same romantic things that I had done with her sister the year before. Some snuggling, some hand holding, and a lot of kissing. Then it happened. One of the biggest misunderstandings of my teenage years.

She had told a friend at one of my porch parties that I had made a pass at her, which I suppose with my naiveté, I thought was some horrible dastardly deed. I got embarrassed and upset. I asked Beth, how could you say that? She looked at me like I was nuts. It was blown way out of proportion. It also didn't help that her phraseology was slightly off. She said that I had made a passover at her. She obviously thought it meant one thing and I thought it meant something sexually bad.

To this day I don't recall the two of us talking it over, trying to make up. I think after that party and my over-exaggerated response, the twins must have thought I was a nut case or something. They would smile and wave, but we had no real conversations. And certainly nothing romantic took place.

I cherished those memories of '78 and '79. When I was younger, I could make friends with girls much easier than I can with women today. Whether I've lost confidence over the years, or it's just bad luck, my last several girlfriends have been nowhere close to being a match for me. One day I hope to meet my soul mate, who I will spend the rest of my life with. As for now, I'm just a middle-aged bachelor having fun writing and looking forward to next year's camp season.

Monsoon Pontoon Ride - It was August of 2010 when, on a late afternoon boat ride, the weather became so foul so quickly it made me feel like one of the passengers on the *S.S. Minnow* from *Gilligan's Island.* Dave and his family had invited me on their rented pontoon boat for a pleasure ride. Although it was somewhat cloudy, the weather was by no means threatening. One by one, David's family and I all met at the dock with chips, dip, soda, and other goodies, ready to be stowed aboard. With a boat full of people and snacks, we were not going to have much speed. This rented pontoon was not built for speed; it was for taking a lot of people on the water for pleasure rides or fishing.

We left the Harvey's dock around 4 p.m. on our way to a spot in between Otter and Oak Islands. After a brisk seven to ten minute ride, we got to our spot, and broke out the snacks and drinks. The first thirty minutes or so were lovely. Good music, good food and sparkling conversation with my family.

Several people took the opportunity to open the side door of the pontoon boat to jump in the lake and cool off. I, of course, not knowing how to swim, was not one of them. I said to Dave, "Don't worry, buddy, I will keep your seat warm for you." Slowly over time we realized that darker, more threatening clouds were forming overhead. I kept an eagle's eye on two ominous looking clouds that had formed. I knew from experience that in Maine, weather could change quickly.

It was approximately 4:30 when the first few faint rumbles of thunder clapped. We all looked around and noticed that on the other side of the lake there still seemed to be a few sunny spots in the sky. We debated as to whether to move there or simply call it a day and head toward camp. Before we could bring it to a vote, a second much louder clap of thunder made the decision for us. We decided that we were going to head in. The anchor was raised, the engine started, and everyone took their seats just as the first few drops of rain began. I remember thinking to myself that we would be into shore before the worst of the storm got there. Boy was I wrong.

All of the sudden the heavens opened up and a torrential downpour pelted everyone on board. The canvas top was down, which made things worse. We had two choices. Stop and try to put it up, or just keep going. The decision was made not to bother with it and focus our attention on getting back to camp.

As it has been said many times, hindsight is 20/20. I was one of the only riders fully clothed. Knowing that I wasn't going to go into the water, I figured why bother putting on a bathing suit. With a hard rain and a moderate wind people were throwing one another towels, wraps, hats … anything they could use for some protection. Soaked to the bone and freezing in my wet clothes, I cowered under my towel, counting the minutes until the ride was over.

As it turned out, the heavy rain made it almost impossible to see. We had to slow down, making the torturous ride even longer. I heard Dave's familiar voice call to me, saying something like, how you doing under there, Joe?

I remember laughing. It seemed a weird question. I was wet, cold, and drenched. How did he think I was doing? Then of course I realized we were all that way. Any answer I gave him would have just sounded silly, so I simply uttered, "Fine!"

As chance would have it, the rain let up just as we were getting ready to dock. I'm not certain but I think a couple of people were going to come out and look for us if we didn't return soon. One by one off stepped nine soggy passengers from the boat. I noticed as I walked up the dock that my shoes squished. Though I could change into clean dry clothes, those shoes were the only pair I brought. I think Dave loaned me a pair of his for the evening, as my soggies dried out by the heater overnight. The next day they finished drying in the warm August sun on my camp's porch.

This summer we did take another pleasure pontoon ride with much better weather. The same group of people, the same good music, but luckily Mother Nature held off her fury.

TRIBUTE TO CAMPERS WHO ARE NO LONGER WITH US

I wish to take some time to let other people know about some of my wonderful friends who are no longer with us. In my first Bear Spring Camps book, I used the phrase 'my mom's crowd' on a few occasions. My mother's crowd has either passed away or is not able to come anymore due to health issues. This story is a tribute to those people.

Malcolm Deacon: My fondest memory of Mr. Deacon is of him sitting on his porch every afternoon, smiling and waving to us kids as we played ball in the old parking area. Always with a friendly hello, he would ask us how we were doing, and we could see it in his eyes that he hoped we would ask him something about fishing or his experiences at Bear Spring.

Mr. Deacon loved pickerel. Many a time people who caught one would bring it in and give it to Mr. Deacon for his supper. He was always most appreciative.

He had an old black Mercedes Benz. I loved that car. When he was able, he would drive it up to the main house himself. In the last few years of his life, his son came with him and would get him to and from meals.

The last year I remember Mr. Deacon being there he was elderly and beginning to have memory issues. When I walked up to him to say hello on the first day, I could tell he knew who I was but my name escaped him and it upset him greatly. He started to get teary eyed. I told him not to worry, and that loving smile came back to his face.

Marion and Jack Feldman: Mr. and Mrs. Feldman arrived at Bear Spring every June and stayed until the camp closed in September. Campers for many years, they had their own boat and their own cabin. Rumor has it that no one else stayed in that cabin from the opening of camp in May until when they arrived in June.

They would always arrive at meals dressed up. As I remember, they would color coordinate their outfits so that his sweater and her blouse would match. They lived in New Jersey but had their mail sent to camp every day during summer. That is a memory that is vivid to me. We sat next to them for years. As I walked into the dining room, I would always see a stack of envelopes at their table and usually, except for an occasional postcard or two, see nothing at ours.

The Feldmans were avid fishermen. When I knew them, they would be out by nine o'clock every morning and not come back in until noon. Although never venturing out of North Bay, they always seemed to catch good sized fish. As I recall, their favorite spots were the two markers and the Boy Scout Camp.

In 1981, when I saw the movie *On Golden Pond*, it reminded me so much of Bear Spring Camps. I was also reminded of the Feldmans, though Jack was not a crotchety old man like the character Norman Thayer. Marion, with her sweet nature, was closer to the character of Ethel. I suppose I thought of the Feldmans during that film more than anyone else, because the Feldmans came to their camp by the lake and stayed all summer. They also shared the love that the Thayers showed for one another.

Today, on the porch of the main house sits a wooden bench in the Feldmans' honor.

Gert and Dick Joyce: The Joyces were also long-time friends of my mother, David, and me. The Joyces enjoyed socializing with all their friends and hosted a Happy Hour every year. When the Joyces would visit Mr. and Mrs. Russell, they would sit on the Russells' porch for hours talking about old times. The younger generation is more into fishing; I don't ever recall Mr. Joyce being a fisherman though he may have been earlier in life.

He pitched in the Benefit Softball game along with Mr. Pearl, the long-time head cook. When I threw my porch party in Mom's honor, the year she passed away, I remember Mr. Joyce coming to my table to tell me that they certainly would have attended but they couldn't get out of their prior engagement. I always thought that was extremely kind of him to let me know that. I knew that he and his wife cared about my mom.

Al and Jean Bennett: Al and Jean Bennett are two of my friends who recently stopped coming to Bear Spring. They were always early risers and part of the 'firstest of the first' breakfast crowd. I would always be greeted by a cheerful, "Hi, Joey," and a warm smile as Mr. Bennett would purchase his morning paper.

In the earlier days when I would walk down to Uncle Cy Greco's cabin in the afternoons, I would see Mr. Bennett sitting in his lawn chair doing a jigsaw puzzle. That is how he liked to relax.

Jean Bennett, along with Mrs. Smarz, was in charge of the camp contribution box for the Benefit Softball game and she was also the score keeper of the ball game.

I was very sad to hear a couple of years ago that the Bennetts were not going to come to Bear Spring anymore. I am glad they are still alive, but miss them at camp. There are many Bennetts from younger generations who continue coming to this day; Rick and Kathy, Brandy, Kyle and Alexa, among many others.

Yes, the Bennetts are a multi-generational family. I believe that members of the Bennett family will continue to come to Bear Spring for many years. I have known many of the younger clan all their lives. When Brandy was an early teenager, we attempted to record a fireside chat. Although it started out with promise, she was called away before we had gotten very far.

Peggy and Bob Smarz: Another wonderful family is the Smarz'. Bob and Peg, Pa and Ma as I affectionately called them, are no longer with us. I am still in close contact with her daughter Sue and I ask how the family is doing as often as I can. I can recall many times visiting Mrs. Smarz on their porch as we talked about the year that had just gone by, as we looked out onto the lake. She had a wonderful sense of humor as did Mr. Smarz. They both loved to laugh. They enjoyed life and lived it to the fullest. I can still hear Ma say to me, "Hi, Joey, how are ya?"

Mr. Smarz once showed me his ten-second fish-catching method. He was with Uncle Cy, Dave, and me on the *Galileo* by the second marker. His magic bait was a worm. He let the line go over the boat so that the worm could sink all the way to the bottom. Once there, he counted to ten. Lo and behold, when he set the hook, he indeed had a fish. I was in hysterics. Coincidence, I thought. It must be. Then he did it again. And a third time. And a fourth. After the fourth fish, he announced, chuckling, "Actually I had that one on two, Joe."

This to me is one of my fondest memories of Mr. Smarz; certainly as a fishing companion. He enjoyed seeing me laugh.

Another wonderful memory of the Smarz' ironically has nothing to do with Bear Spring. A dozen years ago or so, I began calling them at their home in Connecticut every Thanksgiving, Christmas and Easter. They always looked forward to the call. Though it would only last a few minutes, it would bring joy to all of us to hear a familiar camp voice. I miss them very much.

Cy Greco: My mom's dear friend Cy Greco was my uncle for all intents and purposes. Though not related by blood or marriage, to me it didn't matter - he was Uncle Cy. In the early years before Dave started coming up, Uncle Cy would take me fishing in his camp boat. He owned a 1950s Johnson six horse-power engine. Many a time I would ride down to Belgrade Lakes with him to pick up the engine at the marina, and once back at camp, the motor would be installed by a cabin boy.

Uncle Cy told me stories of when he and Aunt Bessie first began coming to Bear Spring. The two of them would ride around the lake checking out every nook and cranny, in the camp boat which had a whopping three and a half horse-power engine. He said, "And you can just imagine how long that took."

The first two years, they didn't fish. They just went exploring up and down the shore lines, looking for good places for fish to hide.

Uncle Cy stayed for a month; the whole month of August. He mentioned to me more than once that he didn't feel as pressured to get everything done, as some people do who only stay a week or two. He had plenty of time to fish, sit inside on a rainy day and read a book, and even partake of a round of miniature golf or two. In the mid-1980s, Uncle Cy, David and I had a miniature-golf tournament. One round and the winner got to hold on to a #1 Golfer coffee mug. Ironically, although I purchased the mug, only Mr. Greco and Dave ever won it.

In 1979, when Uncle Cy retired from being a pharmacist, he sold his business and promised the new folks that he would work for them for a year. I was stunned the day I got to camp and learned that my Uncle Cy wouldn't be there that year. I began calling him every other Saturday promptly at 11 a.m. The following year, even though he did return to camp, the phone calls became a weekly occurrence. We both looked forward to chatting about the week's events for about thirty minutes.

Mr. Greco's last year was 1987, though he lived many years after that. We chatted every Saturday morning right until the end, reminiscing about camp stories and his life.

Bob and Carol Russell: Mr. and Mrs. Russell were our camp neighbors on the left-hand side of my mom's cabin. While they still go to camp as far as I know, they arrive the day that I leave, so I no longer get to see them. I miss them very much which is why I am including them in this story.

Always very warm and friendly, they would arrive at camp with their Boston whaler boat. They would make the rounds, saying hello to all their friends, before they would have that traditional first boat ride of the year. Mr. Russell enjoyed fishing and went out most mornings. Uncle Cy, David and I, in the *Galileo*, would see him out there on the lake, for he frequented the same spots that we did. Only once was I aboard Mr. Russell's boat, which had a humongous engine on it. I remember the bow lifting up so high I couldn't see over it. I looked back toward camp and the cabins were getting smaller by the second. One time I was told the *Galileo's* top speed was twenty-two miles an hour; by my visual estimate, Mr. Russell's boat was at least ten miles an hour faster.

Like many of the campers of my mom's generation, they, too, held a Happy Hour. It was always eagerly anticipated and went well into the early evening.

The Russells had four children, three daughters and a son; Kate, Sue, Kristin, and Michael. All of them are wonderful people. I remember them as kind and courteous, with a fun-loving nature.

Marguerite and Bertram Mosher Jr.: Bert Mosher owned and ran Bear Spring Camps when I was a child. His daughter Peg and her husband Ron are now in charge.

Mrs. Marguerite Mosher sadly passed away in March of 2012. My memories of her are of a loving human being, always with the kind word and warm smile. Though she was out of the business end of the camp for many years, she was not hard to find, and always enjoyed a good conversation.

Although I got this memory second-hand from Uncle Cy, it definitely tickled my funny bone. One year Central Maine was in the thick of a major heat wave with temperatures at least fifteen degrees warmer than usual. Mrs. Mosher was not pleased and remarked to Uncle Cy, "I don't know how you folks put up with this heat down in New York. This is brutal."

Memories of Mr. Mosher include him riding his lawn tractor to mow the grass, driving up and down the lane in the old, blue, camp pickup truck, and his cheerful way as he greeted his beloved customers who were more like family to him. He was always willing to go the extra mile to tell people something they needed to know, like the time he came down to the clearing to let us know that the bridge had washed out. On a lighter note, he was also the honorary coach of the Moshers Maulers, the staff softball team. Mr. George Knox, another long-time camper of whom I have fond memories, was the honorary coach of the Knox's Goldbricks, the camper softball team. Mr. Knox occupied the cabin to our right. Bert passed away in 1987.

***

Unbeknownst to me when I was young, my emotional system was harder to control because of my Cerebral Palsy. Even after my teenage years, I still had to fight my emotions. I always felt extremely sad and cried when I had to leave my friends at camp. To me they are my family. One time when I went to say good-bye to Joan Sullivan, the daughter of another fine camp family, she hugged me as if to say I know exactly how you feel.

Nowadays when saying goodbye to people, I don't outwardly show my emotions, however the love I feel for the aforementioned people, as well as the current group of campers who still attend Bear Spring, is exactly the same. I now have tools in place to better cope with the sad situation of leaving.

There are many, many other fine people I have known over the years, too numerous to mention; that does not diminish their importance to me. Bear Spring Camps and the people who go there will be a part of my life that I will cherish forever, and I am quite certain I will reminisce over the old camp stories for years to come.

THE END

ABOUT THE AUTHOR

Joseph M. Kockelmans lives in central Pennsylvania. This is his second published book. He previously wrote and published *Picking Up Where We Left Off: My Bear Spring Camps Stories*. He has also written a play, *Kimberly*, which had a staged reading by performers at the Cresson Lake Playhouse Theatre. He started going to Bear Spring Camps in 1970 when he was five years old and still attends the camp every year during the first week in August.

CPSIA information can be obtained at www.ICGtesting.com
Printed in the USA
LVOW12s2048290814

401520LV00001B/73/P